Declaring

to

SEAP

Daily devotional

guide to becoming a better you

Declaring

to

SEAP

Daily devotional
guide to becoming a better you

Jacqui J.

Declaring to SEAP

Daily devotional
guide to becoming a better you

Declaring to SEAP - a 40- day daily devotional (guide to becoming a better you) - provides you with an opportunity to be encouraged, inspired and establish personal growth through your daily devotions. Each devotion contains scriptures, real goal setting opportunities, and reflective check-ins. Each devotional contains SEAP - spiritual (self care), emotional, academic and physical goal setting and a reflective *check-in. Ready, Set and Go – start your journey to becoming a better you.*

Declaring to SEAP Devotional

Declaring a Spiritual/Self-Care, Emotional, Academic and Physical Increase...

> **James 1:5**
> *If any of you lacks wisdom, you should ask God, who gives generously to all without finding fault, and it will be given to you.*

*I declare today **Spiritually** I will ...*

_____

_____

*I declare today through **Self-Care** I will ...*

_____

_____

*I declare today that **Emotionally** I will …*

_____

_____

*I declare today that **Academically** I will …*

_____

_____

*I declare today that **Physically** I will …*

_____

_____

Daily Reflection

As you reflect on your declarations, what did you do and why did you do it?
(Ex. I did..., Indicate what you did to become a better you in each area.)

Spiritually/Self-Care _____

_____

Emotionally _____

_____

Academically _____

_____

Physically _____

_____

How do you feel about your increase?

Declaring to SEAP Devotional

Declaring a Spiritual/Self-Care, Emotional, Academic and Physical Increase...

Isaiah 26:3
You will keep in perfect peace those whose minds are steadfast, because they trust in you.

---

*I declare today **Spiritually** I will ...*

_____

_____

*I declare today through **Self-Care** I will ...*

_____

_____

*I declare today that **Emotionally** I will ...*

_____

_____

*I declare today that **Academically** I will ...*

_____

_____

*I declare today that **Physically** I will ...*

_____

_____

Daily Reflection

As you reflect on your declarations, what did you do and why did you do it?
(Ex. I did..., Indicate what you did to become a better you in each area.)

Spiritually/Self-Care _____

_____

Emotionally _____

_____

Academically _____

_____

Physically _____

_____

How do you feel about your increase?

Declaring to SEAP Devotional

Declaring a Spiritual/Self-Care, Emotional, Academic and Physical Increase...

---

2 Thessalonians 3:16
Now may the Lord of peace himself give you peace at all times and in every way. The Lord be with all of you.

---

*I declare today **Spiritually** I will ...*

_____

_____

*I declare today through **Self-Care** I will ...*

_____

_____

*I declare today that **Emotionally** I will ...*

_____

_____

*I declare today that **Academically** I will ...*

_____

_____

*I declare today that **Physically** I will ...*

_____

_____

Daily Reflection

As you reflect on your declarations, what did you do and why did you do it?
(Ex. I did..., Indicate what you did to become a better you in each area.)

Spiritually/Self-Care _____

_____

Emotionally _____

_____

Academically _____

_____

Physically _____

_____

How do you feel about your increase?

Declaring to SEAP Devotional

Declaring a Spiritual/Self-Care, Emotional, Academic and Physical Increase...

John 16:33
"I have told you these things, so that in me you may have peace. In this world you will have trouble. But take heart! I have overcome the world."

---

*I declare today **Spiritually** I will ...*

_____

_____

*I declare today through **Self-Care** I will ...*

_____

_____

*I declare today that **Emotionally** I will ...*

_____

_____

*I declare today that **Academically** I will ...*

_____

_____

*I declare today that **Physically** I will ...*

_____

_____

Daily Reflection

As you reflect on your declarations, what did you do and why did you do it?
(Ex. I did..., Indicate what you did to become a better you in each area.)

Spiritually/Self-Care _____

_____

Emotionally _____

_____

Academically _____

_____

Physically _____

_____

How do you feel about your increase?

Declaring to SEAP Devotional

Declaring a Spiritual/Self-Care, Emotional, Academic and Physical Increase...

> ### *1 Peter 5:7*
> *Cast all your anxiety on him because he cares for you.*

*I declare today **Spiritually** I will ...*

_____

_____

*I declare today through **Self-Care** I will ...*

_____

_____

*I declare today that **Emotionally** I will ...*

_____

_____

*I declare today that **Academically** I will ...*

_____

_____

*I declare today that **Physically** I will ...*

_____

_____

Daily Reflection

As you reflect on your declarations, what did you do and why did you do it?
(Ex. I did..., Indicate what you did to become a better you in each area.)

Spiritually/Self-Care _____

_____

Emotionally _____

_____

Academically _____

_____

Physically _____

_____

How do you feel about your increase?

Declaring to SEAP Devotional

Declaring a Spiritual/Self-Care, Emotional, Academic and Physical Increase...

Philippians 4:6
Do not be anxious about anything, but in every situation, by prayer and petition, with thanksgiving, present your requests to God.

I declare today **Spiritually** *I will ...*

_____

_____

I declare today through **Self-Care** *I will ...*

_____

_____

*I declare today that **Emotionally** I will ...*

_____

_____

*I declare today that **Academically** I will ...*

_____

_____

*I declare today that **Physically** I will ...*

_____

_____

Daily Reflection

As you reflect on your declarations, what did you do and why did you do it?
(Ex. I did..., Indicate what you did to become a better you in each area.)

Spiritually/Self-Care _____

_____

Emotionally _____

_____

Academically _____

_____

Physically _____

_____

How do you feel about your increase?

Declaring to SEAP Devotional

Declaring a Spiritual/Self-Care, Emotional, Academic and Physical Increase...

Philippians 4:7
And the peace of God, which transcends all understanding, will guard your hearts and your minds in Christ Jesus.

---

*I declare today **Spiritually** I will ...*

_____

_____

*I declare today through **Self-Care** I will ...*

_____

_____

*I declare today that **Emotionally** I will ...*

_____

_____

*I declare today that **Academically** I will ...*

_____

_____

*I declare today that **Physically** I will ...*

_____

_____

Daily Reflection

As you reflect on your declarations, what did you do and why did you do it?
(Ex. I did..., Indicate what you did to become a better you in each area.)

Spiritually/Self-Care _____

_____

Emotionally _____

_____

Academically _____

_____

Physically _____

_____

How do you feel about your increase?

Declaring to SEAP Devotional

Declaring a Spiritual/Self-Care, Emotional, Academic and Physical Increase...

Philippians 1:9-10

And this is my prayer: that your love may abound more and more in knowledge and depth of insight, 10) so that you may be able to discern what is best and may be pure and blameless for the day of Christ.

---

*I declare today **Spiritually** I will ...*

_____

_____

*I declare today through **Self-Care** I will ...*

_____

_____

*I declare today that **Emotionally** I will ...*

_____

_____

*I declare today that **Academically** I will ...*

_____

_____

*I declare today that **Physically** I will ...*

_____

_____

Daily Reflection

As you reflect on your declarations, what did you do and why did you do it?
(Ex. I did..., Indicate what you did to become a better you in each area.)

Spiritually/Self-Care _____

_____

Emotionally _____

_____

Academically _____

_____

Physically _____

_____

How do you feel about your increase?

Declaring to SEAP Devotional

Declaring a Spiritual/Self-Care, Emotional, Academic and Physical Increase...

---

2 Timothy 2:15
Do your best to present yourself to God as one approved, a worker who does not need to be ashamed and who correctly handles the word of truth.

---

*I declare today **Spiritually** I will ...*

_____

_____

*I declare today through **Self-Care** I will ...*

_____

_____

*I declare today that **Emotionally** I will ...*

_____

_____

*I declare today that **Academically** I will ...*

_____

_____

*I declare today that **Physically** I will ...*

_____

_____

Daily Reflection

As you reflect on your declarations, what did you do and why did you do it?
(Ex. I did..., Indicate what you did to become a better you in each area.)

Spiritually/Self-Care _____

_____

Emotionally _____

_____

Academically _____

_____

Physically _____

_____

How do you feel about your increase?

Declaring to SEAP Devotional

Declaring a Spiritual/Self-Care, Emotional, Academic and Physical Increase...

Ephesians 2:10
For we are God's handiwork, created in Christ Jesus to do good works, which God prepared in advance for us to do.

I declare today **Spiritually** *I will ...*

_____

_____

I declare today through **Self-Care** *I will ...*

_____

_____

*I declare today that **Emotionally** I will ...*

_____

_____

*I declare today that **Academically** I will ...*

_____

_____

*I declare today that **Physically** I will ...*

_____

_____

Daily Reflection

As you reflect on your declarations, what did you do and why did you do it?
(Ex. I did..., Indicate what you did to become a better you in each area.)

Spiritually/Self-Care _____

_____

Emotionally _____

_____

Academically _____

_____

Physically _____

_____

How do you feel about your increase?

Declaring to SEAP Devotional

Declaring a Spiritual/Self-Care, Emotional, Academic and Physical Increase...

Proverbs 3: 26
for the Lord will be at your side and will keep your foot from being snared.

I declare today **Spiritually** *I will ...*

_____

_____

I declare today through **Self-Care** *I will ...*

_____

_____

*I declare today that **Emotionally** I will ...*

_____

_____

*I declare today that **Academically** I will ...*

_____

_____

*I declare today that **Physically** I will ...*

_____

_____

Daily Reflection

As you reflect on your declarations, what did you do and why did you do it?
(Ex. I did..., Indicate what you did to become a better you in each area.)

Spiritually/Self-Care _____

_____

Emotionally _____

_____

Academically _____

_____

Physically _____

_____

How do you feel about your increase?

Declaring to SEAP Devotional

Declaring a Spiritual/Self-Care, Emotional, Academic and Physical Increase...

> **Philippians 4:13**
> I can do all this through him who gives me strength.

*I declare today **Spiritually** I will ...*

_____

_____

*I declare today through **Self-Care** I will ...*

_____

_____

*I declare today that **Emotionally** I will ...*

_____

_____

*I declare today that **Academically** I will …*

_____

_____

*I declare today that **Physically** I will …*

_____

_____

Daily Reflection

As you reflect on your declarations, what did you do and why did you do it?
(Ex. I did..., Indicate what you did to become a better you in each area.)

Spiritually/Self-Care _____

_____

Emotionally _____

_____

Academically _____

_____

Physically _____

_____

How do you feel about your increase?

Declaring to SEAP Devotional

Declaring a Spiritual/Self-Care, Emotional, Academic and Physical Increase...

Philippians 1:6
Being confident of this, that he who began a good work in you will carry it on to completion until the day of Christ Jesus.

---

*I declare today **Spiritually** I will ...*

_____

_____

*I declare today through **Self-Care** I will ...*

_____

_____

*I declare today that **Emotionally** I will ...*

_____

_____

*I declare today that **Academically** I will ...*

_____

_____

*I declare today that **Physically** I will ...*

_____

_____

Daily Reflection

As you reflect on your declarations, what did you do and why did you do it?
(Ex. I did..., Indicate what you did to become a better you in each area.)

Spiritually/Self-Care _____

_____

Emotionally _____

_____

Academically _____

_____

Physically _____

_____

How do you feel about your increase?

Declaring to SEAP Devotional

Declaring a Spiritual/Self-Care, Emotional, Academic and Physical Increase...

---

1 Corinthians 10:31
So whether you eat or drink or whatever you do, do it all for the glory of God.

---

*I declare today **Spiritually** I will ...*

_____

_____

*I declare today through **Self-Care** I will ...*

_____

_____

*I declare today that **Emotionally** I will ...*

_____

_____

*I declare today that **Academically** I will ...*

_____

_____

*I declare today that **Physically** I will ...*

_____

_____

Daily Reflection

As you reflect on your declarations, what did you do and why did you do it?
(Ex. I did..., Indicate what you did to become a better you in each area.)

Spiritually/Self-Care _____

_____

Emotionally _____

_____

Academically _____

_____

Physically _____

_____

How do you feel about your increase?

Declaring to SEAP Devotional

Declaring a Spiritual/Self-Care, Emotional, Academic and Physical Increase...

Psalms 33:4
For the word of the Lord is right and true; he is faithful in all he does.

---

*I declare today **Spiritually** I will ...*

_____

_____

*I declare today through **Self-Care** I will ...*

_____

_____

*I declare today that **Emotionally** I will ...*

_____

_____

*I declare today that **Academically** I will ...*

_____

_____

*I declare today that **Physically** I will ...*

_____

_____

Daily Reflection

As you reflect on your declarations, what did you do and why did you do it?
(Ex. I did..., Indicate what you did to become a better you in each area.)

Spiritually/Self-Care _____

_____

Emotionally _____

_____

Academically _____

_____

Physically _____

_____

How do you feel about your increase?

Declaring to SEAP Devotional

Declaring a Spiritual/Self-Care, Emotional, Academic and Physical Increase...

Proverbs 3:24
When you lie down, you will not be afraid; when you lie down, your sleep will be sweet.

---

*I declare today **Spiritually** I will ...*

_____

_____

*I declare today through **Self-Care** I will ...*

_____

_____

*I declare today that **Emotionally** I will ...*

_____

_____

*I declare today that **Academically** I will ...*

_____

_____

*I declare today that **Physically** I will ...*

_____

_____

Daily Reflection

As you reflect on your declarations, what did you do and why did you do it?
(Ex. I did..., Indicate what you did to become a better you in each area.)

Spiritually/Self-Care _____

_____

Emotionally _____

_____

Academically _____

_____

Physically _____

_____

How do you feel about your increase?

Declaring to SEAP Devotional

Declaring a Spiritual/Self-Care, Emotional, Academic and Physical Increase...

Psalms 46:1
God is our refuge and strength, an ever-present help in trouble.

---

*I declare today **Spiritually** I will ...*

_____

_____

*I declare today through **Self-Care** I will ...*

_____

_____

*I declare today that **Emotionally** I will ...*

_____

_____

*I declare today that **Academically** I will ...*

_____

_____

*I declare today that **Physically** I will ...*

_____

_____

Daily Reflection

As you reflect on your declarations, what did you do and why did you do it?
(Ex. I did..., Indicate what you did to become a better you in each area.)

Spiritually/Self-Care _____

_____

Emotionally _____

_____

Academically _____

_____

Physically _____

_____

How do you feel about your increase?

Declaring to SEAP Devotional

Declaring a Spiritual/Self-Care, Emotional, Academic and Physical Increase...

Psalms 86:5
You, Lord are forgiving and good, abounding in love to all who call to you.

---

*I declare today **Spiritually** I will ...*

_____

_____

*I declare today through **Self-Care** I will ...*

_____

_____

*I declare today that **Emotionally** I will ...*

_____

_____

*I declare today that **Academically** I will ...*

_____

_____

*I declare today that **Physically** I will ...*

_____

_____

Daily Reflection

As you reflect on your declarations, what did you do and why did you do it?
(Ex. I did..., Indicate what you did to become a better you in each area.)

Spiritually/Self-Care _____

_____

Emotionally _____

_____

Academically _____

_____

Physically _____

_____

How do you feel about your increase?

Declaring to SEAP Devotional

Declaring a Spiritual/Self-Care, Emotional, Academic and Physical Increase...

Psalms 34:8
Taste and see that the Lord is good; blessed is the one who takes refuge in him.

I declare today **Spiritually** *I will ...*

_____

_____

I declare today through **Self-Care** *I will ...*

_____

_____

*I declare today that **Emotionally** I will ...*

_____

_____

*I declare today that **Academically** I will ...*

_____

_____

*I declare today that **Physically** I will ...*

_____

_____

Daily Reflection

As you reflect on your declarations, what did you do and why did you do it?
(Ex. I did..., Indicate what you did to become a better you in each area.)

Spiritually/Self-Care _____

_____

Emotionally _____

_____

Academically _____

_____

Physically _____

_____

How do you feel about your increase?

Declaring to SEAP Devotional

Declaring a Spiritual/Self-Care, Emotional, Academic and Physical Increase...

Psalms 145:9
The Lord is good to all; he has compassion on all he has made.

---

*I declare today **Spiritually** I will ...*

_____

_____

*I declare today through **Self-Care** I will ...*

_____

_____

*I declare today that **Emotionally** I will ...*

_____

_____

*I declare today that **Academically** I will ...*

_____

_____

*I declare today that **Physically** I will ...*

_____

_____

Daily Reflection

As you reflect on your declarations, what did you do and why did you do it?
(Ex. I did..., Indicate what you did to become a better you in each area.)

Spiritually/Self-Care _____

_____

Emotionally _____

_____

Academically _____

_____

Physically _____

_____

How do you feel about your increase?

Declaring to SEAP Devotional

*Declaring a Spiritual/Self-Care,
Emotional, Academic and Physical
Increase...*

Romans 12:12
*Be joyful in hope, patient in affliction, faithful
in prayer.*

I declare today **Spiritually** *I will ...*

_____

_____

I declare today through **Self-Care** *I will ...*

_____

_____

*I declare today that **Emotionally** I will ...*

_____

_____

*I declare today that **Academically** I will ...*

_____

_____

*I declare today that **Physically** I will ...*

_____

_____

Daily Reflection

As you reflect on your declarations, what did you do and why did you do it?
(Ex. I did..., Indicate what you did to become a better you in each area.)

Spiritually/Self-Care _____

_____

Emotionally _____

_____

Academically _____

_____

Physically _____

_____

How do you feel about your increase?

Declaring to SEAP Devotional

Declaring a Spiritual/Self-Care, Emotional, Academic and Physical Increase...

> **Psalms 148:3-5**
> *Praise him, sun and moon; praise him, all you shining stars. 4) Praise him, you highest heavens and you waters above the skies. 5) Let them praise the name of the Lord, for at his command they were created,*

*I declare today **Spiritually** I will ...*

_____

_____

*I declare today through **Self-Care** I will ...*

_____

_____

*I declare today that **Emotionally** I will ...*

_____

_____

*I declare today that **Academically** I will ...*

_____

_____

*I declare today that **Physically** I will ...*

_____

_____

Daily Reflection

As you reflect on your declarations, what did you do and why did you do it?
(Ex. I did..., Indicate what you did to become a better you in each area.)

Spiritually/Self-Care _____

_____

Emotionally _____

_____

Academically _____

_____

Physically _____

_____

How do you feel about your increase?

Declaring to SEAP Devotional

Declaring a Spiritual/Self-Care, Emotional, Academic and Physical Increase...

Romans 15:13

May the God of hope fill you with all joy and peace as you trust in him, so that you may overflow with hope by the power of the Holy Spirit.

I declare today **Spiritually** *I will ...*

_____

_____

I declare today through **Self-Care** *I will ...*

_____

_____

*I declare today that **Emotionally** I will ...*

_____

_____

*I declare today that **Academically** I will ...*

_____

_____

*I declare today that **Physically** I will ...*

_____

_____

Daily Reflection

As you reflect on your declarations, what did you do and why did you do it?
(Ex. I did..., Indicate what you did to become a better you in each area.)

Spiritually/Self-Care _____

_____

Emotionally _____

_____

Academically _____

_____

Physically _____

_____

How do you feel about your increase?

Declaring to SEAP Devotional

Declaring a Spiritual/Self-Care, Emotional, Academic and Physical Increase...

Revelation 4:11

"You are worthy, our Lord and God, to receive glory and honor and power, for you created all things, and by your will they were created and have their being."

---

*I declare today **Spiritually** I will ...*

_____

_____

*I declare today through **Self-Care** I will ...*

_____

_____

*I declare today that **Emotionally** I will ...*

_____

_____

*I declare today that **Academically** I will ...*

_____

_____

*I declare today that **Physically** I will ...*

_____

_____

Daily Reflection

As you reflect on your declarations, what did you do and why did you do it?
(Ex. I did..., Indicate what you did to become a better you in each area.)

Spiritually/Self-Care _____

_____

Emotionally _____

_____

Academically _____

_____

Physically _____

_____

How do you feel about your increase?

Declaring to SEAP Devotional

Declaring a Spiritual/Self-Care, Emotional, Academic and Physical Increase...

Psalms 89:11
The heavens are yours, and yours also the earth; you founded the world and all that is in it.

---

*I declare today **Spiritually** I will ...*

_____

_____

*I declare today through **Self-Care** I will ...*

_____

_____

*I declare today that **Emotionally** I will ...*

_____

_____

*I declare today that **Academically** I will ...*

_____

_____

*I declare today that **Physically** I will ...*

_____

_____

Daily Reflection

As you reflect on your declarations, what did you do and why did you do it?
(Ex. I did..., Indicate what you did to become a better you in each area.)

Spiritually/Self-Care _____

_____

Emotionally _____

_____

Academically _____

_____

Physically _____

_____

How do you feel about your increase?

Declaring to SEAP Devotional

Declaring a Spiritual/Self-Care, Emotional, Academic and Physical Increase...

Psalms 117:2
For great is his love toward us, and the faithfulness of the Lord endures forever. Praise the Lord.

---

*I declare today **Spiritually** I will ...*

_____

_____

*I declare today through **Self-Care** I will ...*

_____

_____

*I declare today that **Emotionally** I will ...*

_____

_____

*I declare today that **Academically** I will ...*

_____

_____

*I declare today that **Physically** I will ...*

_____

_____

Daily Reflection

As you reflect on your declarations, what did you do and why did you do it?
(Ex. I did..., Indicate what you did to become a better you in each area.)

Spiritually/Self-Care _____

_____

Emotionally _____

_____

Academically _____

_____

Physically _____

_____

How do you feel about your increase?

Declaring to SEAP Devotional

Declaring a Spiritual/Self-Care, Emotional, Academic and Physical Increase...

---

1 Corinthians 13:13
And now these three remain: faith, hope, and love. But the greatest of these is love.

---

*I declare today **Spiritually** I will ...*

_____

_____

*I declare today through **Self-Care** I will ...*

_____

_____

*I declare today that **Emotionally** I will ...*

_____

_____

*I declare today that **Academically** I will ...*

_____

_____

*I declare today that **Physically** I will ...*

_____

_____

Daily Reflection

As you reflect on your declarations, what did you do and why did you do it?
(Ex. I did..., Indicate what you did to become a better you in each area.)

Spiritually/Self-Care _____

_____

Emotionally _____

_____

Academically _____

_____

Physically _____

_____

How do you feel about your increase?

Declaring to SEAP Devotional

*Declaring a Spiritual/Self-Care,
Emotional, Academic and Physical
Increase...*

Isaiah 40:31
*But those who hope in the Lord will renew their
strength. They will soar on wings like eagles;
they will run and not grown weary, they will
walk and not be faint,*

---

*I declare today **Spiritually** I will ...*

_____

_____

*I declare today through **Self-Care** I will ...*

_____

_____

*I declare today that **Emotionally** I will ...*

_____

_____

*I declare today that **Academically** I will ...*

_____

_____

*I declare today that **Physically** I will ...*

_____

_____

Daily Reflection

As you reflect on your declarations, what did you do and why did you do it?
(Ex. I did..., Indicate what you did to become a better you in each area.)

Spiritually/Self-Care _____

_____

Emotionally _____

_____

Academically _____

_____

Physically _____

_____

How do you feel about your increase?

Declaring to SEAP Devotional

*Declaring a Spiritual/Self-Care,
Emotional, Academic and Physical
Increase...*

---

1 Corinthians 15:58
*Therefore, my dear brothers and sisters, stand
firm. Let nothing move you. Always give
yourselves fully to the work of the Lord,
because you know that your labor in the Lord
is not in vain.*

---

*I declare today **Spiritually** I will ...*

_____

_____

*I declare today through **Self-Care** I will ...*

_____

_____

*I declare today that **Emotionally** I will ...*

_____

_____

*I declare today that **Academically** I will ...*

_____

_____

*I declare today that **Physically** I will ...*

_____

_____

Daily Reflection

As you reflect on your declarations, what did you do and why did you do it?
(Ex. I did..., Indicate what you did to become a better you in each area.)

Spiritually/Self-Care _____

_____

Emotionally _____

_____

Academically _____

_____

Physically _____

_____

How do you feel about your increase?

Declaring to SEAP Devotional

Declaring a Spiritual/Self-Care, Emotional, Academic and Physical Increase...

Psalms 118:7
The Lord is with me; he is my helper. I look in triumph on my enemies.

---

*I declare today **Spiritually** I will ...*

_____

_____

*I declare today through **Self-Care** I will ...*

_____

_____

*I declare today that **Emotionally** I will ...*

_____

_____

*I declare today that **Academically** I will ...*

_____

_____

*I declare today that **Physically** I will ...*

_____

_____

Daily Reflection

As you reflect on your declarations, what did you do and why did you do it?
(Ex. I did..., Indicate what you did to become a better you in each area.)

Spiritually/Self-Care _____

_____

Emotionally _____

_____

Academically _____

_____

Physically _____

_____

How do you feel about your increase?

Declaring to SEAP Devotional

Declaring a Spiritual/Self-Care, Emotional, Academic and Physical Increase...

Psalms 91:1
Whoever dwells in the shelter of the Most High will rest in the shadow of the Almighty.

---

*I declare today **Spiritually** I will ...*

_____

_____

*I declare today through **Self-Care** I will ...*

_____

_____

*I declare today that **Emotionally** I will ...*

_____

_____

*I declare today that **Academically** I will ...*

_____

_____

*I declare today that **Physically** I will ...*

_____

_____

Daily Reflection

As you reflect on your declarations, what did you do and why did you do it?
(Ex. I did..., Indicate what you did to become a better you in each area.)

Spiritually/Self-Care _____

_____

Emotionally _____

_____

Academically _____

_____

Physically _____

_____

How do you feel about your increase?

*Declaring to SEAP Devotional

Declaring a Spiritual/Self-Care, Emotional, Academic and Physical Increase...

Psalms 118:8
It is better to take refuge in the Lord than to trust in humans.

I declare today **Spiritually** I will ...

_____

_____

I declare today through **Self-Care** I will ...

_____

_____

*I declare today that **Emotionally** I will ...*

_____

_____

*I declare today that **Academically** I will ...*

_____

_____

*I declare today that **Physically** I will ...*

_____

_____

Daily Reflection

As you reflect on your declarations, what did you do and why did you do it?
(Ex. I did..., Indicate what you did to become a better you in each area.)

Spiritually/Self-Care _____

_____

Emotionally _____

_____

Academically _____

_____

Physically _____

_____

How do you feel about your increase?

Declaring to SEAP Devotional

Declaring a Spiritual/Self-Care, Emotional, Academic and Physical Increase...

Psalms 121:7
The Lord will keep you from all harm - he will watch over your life;

*I declare today **Spiritually** I will ...*

_____

_____

*I declare today through **Self-Care** I will ...*

_____

_____

*I declare today that **Emotionally** I will ...*

_____

_____

*I declare today that **Academically** I will ...*

_____

_____

*I declare today that **Physically** I will ...*

_____

_____

Daily Reflection

*As you reflect on your declarations, what
did you do and why did you do it?*
**(Ex. I did..., Indicate what you did to become a
better you in each area.)**

Spiritually/Self-Care _____

_____

Emotionally _____

_____

Academically _____

_____

Physically _____

_____

How do you feel about your increase?

Declaring to SEAP Devotional

Declaring a Spiritual/Self-Care, Emotional, Academic and Physical Increase...

Jeremiah 29:11
For I know the plans I have for you," declares the Lord, "plans to prosper you and not to harm you, plans to give you hope and a future.

---

*I declare today **Spiritually** I will ...*

_____

_____

*I declare today through **Self-Care** I will ...*

_____

_____

*I declare today that **Emotionally** I will ...*

_____

_____

*I declare today that **Academically** I will ...*

_____

_____

*I declare today that **Physically** I will ...*

_____

_____

Daily Reflection

As you reflect on your declarations, what did you do and why did you do it?
(Ex. I did..., Indicate what you did to become a better you in each area.)

Spiritually/Self-Care _____

_____

Emotionally _____

_____

Academically _____

_____

Physically _____

_____

How do you feel about your increase?

Declaring to SEAP Devotional

Declaring a Spiritual/Self-Care, Emotional, Academic and Physical Increase...

> **Hebrews 11:1**
> *Now faith is confidence in what we hope for and assurance about what we do not see.*

*I declare today **Spiritually** I will ...*

_____

_____

*I declare today through **Self-Care** I will ...*

_____

_____

*I declare today that **Emotionally** I will ...*

_____

_____

*I declare today that **Academically** I will ...*

_____

_____

*I declare today that **Physically** I will ...*

_____

_____

Daily Reflection

As you reflect on your declarations, what did you do and why did you do it?
(Ex. I did..., Indicate what you did to become a better you in each area.)

Spiritually/Self-Care _____

_____

Emotionally _____

_____

Academically _____

_____

Physically _____

_____

How do you feel about your increase?

Declaring to SEAP Devotional

*Declaring a Spiritual/Self-Care,
Emotional, Academic and Physical
Increase...*

> **1 Corinthians 13:13**
> *And now these three remain: faith, hope and
> love. But the greatest of these is love.*

*I declare today **Spiritually** I will ...*

_____

_____

*I declare today through **Self-Care** I will ...*

_____

_____

*I declare today that **Emotionally** I will …*

_____

_____

*I declare today that **Academically** I will …*

_____

_____

*I declare today that **Physically** I will …*

_____

_____

Daily Reflection

As you reflect on your declarations, what did you do and why did you do it?
(Ex. I did..., Indicate what you did to become a better you in each area.)

Spiritually/Self-Care _____

_____

Emotionally _____

_____

Academically _____

_____

Physically _____

_____

How do you feel about your increase?

Declaring to SEAP Devotional

Declaring a Spiritual/Self-Care, Emotional, Academic and Physical Increase...

Psalms 31:24
Be strong and take heart, all you who hope in the Lord.

---

*I declare today **Spiritually** I will ...*

_____

_____

*I declare today through **Self-Care** I will ...*

_____

_____

*I declare today that **Emotionally** I will ...*

_____

_____

*I declare today that **Academically** I will ...*

_____

_____

*I declare today that **Physically** I will ...*

_____

_____

Daily Reflection

As you reflect on your declarations, what did you do and why did you do it?
(Ex. I did..., Indicate what you did to become a better you in each area.)

Spiritually/Self-Care _____

_____

Emotionally _____

_____

Academically _____

_____

Physically _____

_____

How do you feel about your increase?

Declaring to SEAP Devotional

Declaring a Spiritual/Self-Care, Emotional, Academic and Physical Increase...

> **Psalms 62:5**
> *Yes, my soul, find rest in God; my hope comes from him.*

I declare today **Spiritually** *I will ...*

_____

_____

I declare today through **Self-Care** *I will ...*

_____

_____

*I declare today that **Emotionally** I will ...*

_____

_____

*I declare today that **Academically** I will ...*

_____

_____

*I declare today that **Physically** I will ...*

_____

_____

Daily Reflection

As you reflect on your declarations, what did you do and why did you do it?
(Ex. I did..., Indicate what you did to become a better you in each area.)

Spiritually/Self-Care _____

_____

Emotionally _____

_____

Academically _____

_____

Physically _____

_____

How do you feel about your increase?

Declaring to SEAP Devotional

Declaring a Spiritual/Self-Care, Emotional, Academic and Physical Increase...

Psalms 39:7
"But now, Lord, what do I look for? My hope is in you.

---

*I declare today **Spiritually** I will ...*

_____

_____

*I declare today through **Self-Care** I will ...*

_____

_____

*I declare today that **Emotionally** I will ...*

_____

_____

*I declare today that **Academically** I will ...*

_____

_____

*I declare today that **Physically** I will ...*

_____

_____

Daily Reflection

As you reflect on your declarations, what did you do and why did you do it?
(Ex. I did..., Indicate what you did to become a better you in each area.)

Spiritually/Self-Care _____

_____

Emotionally _____

_____

Academically _____

_____

Physically _____

_____

How do you feel about your increase?

Declaring to SEAP Devotional

Declaring a Spiritual/Self-Care, Emotional, Academic and Physical Increase...

Declare today and always to SEAP, invest in yourself, always be emotionally connected while increasing academic abilities that will allow you to apply wisdom in all areas of your life. Additionally, maintaining a physical connection with yourself where you are able to intentionally build awareness for your physical being.

Daily SEAP is one of the best investments one can make in this life. Understanding the need of yourself and declaring to SEAP can reward you with a wealth of becoming a better you.

DECLARE
TO
SEAP!

SEAP

Declaring to
Spiritually/Self-Care,
Emotionally, Academically
And
Physically
Aware of needs in order to
create a better you!

SEAP

This daily devotional provides you an opportunity to reflect and grow.

Enjoy the journey and SEAP!

Spiritually/Self Care

Emotionally

Academically

And

Physically

*Become a better you
daily.*

Resources

The Holy Bible, New International Version® NIV ® Copyright © 1973, 1978, 1984, 2011 by Biblica, Inc. ® Used by Permission of Biblica, Inc. ® All rights reserved worldwide.

www.ingramcontent.com/pod-product-compliance
Lightning Source LLC
Chambersburg PA
CBHW060328050426
42449CB00011B/2701